I0014186

Syed Nawaz
Sampa Sahoo
Bibhudatta Sahoo

Real Time Tasks Scheduling in Cloud Computing Environment

Syed Nawaz
Sampa Sahoo
Bibhudatta Sahoo

Real Time Tasks Scheduling in Cloud Computing Environment

Scholar's Press

Impressum / Imprint
Bibliografische Information der Deutschen Nationalbibliothek: Die Deutsche Nationalbibliothek verzeichnet diese Publikation in der Deutschen Nationalbibliografie; detaillierte bibliografische Daten sind im Internet über http://dnb.d-nb.de abrufbar.
Alle in diesem Buch genannten Marken und Produktnamen unterliegen warenzeichen-, marken- oder patentrechtlichem Schutz bzw. sind Warenzeichen oder eingetragene Warenzeichen der jeweiligen Inhaber. Die Wiedergabe von Marken, Produktnamen, Gebrauchsnamen, Handelsnamen, Warenbezeichnungen u.s.w. in diesem Werk berechtigt auch ohne besondere Kennzeichnung nicht zu der Annahme, dass solche Namen im Sinne der Warenzeichen- und Markenschutzgesetzgebung als frei zu betrachten wären und daher von jedermann benutzt werden dürften.

Bibliographic information published by the Deutsche Nationalbibliothek: The Deutsche Nationalbibliothek lists this publication in the Deutsche Nationalbibliografie; detailed bibliographic data are available in the Internet at http://dnb.d-nb.de.
Any brand names and product names mentioned in this book are subject to trademark, brand or patent protection and are trademarks or registered trademarks of their respective holders. The use of brand names, product names, common names, trade names, product descriptions etc. even without a particular marking in this work is in no way to be construed to mean that such names may be regarded as unrestricted in respect of trademark and brand protection legislation and could thus be used by anyone.

Coverbild / Cover image: www.ingimage.com

Verlag / Publisher:
Scholar's Press
ist ein Imprint der / is a trademark of
OmniScriptum GmbH & Co. KG
Heinrich-Böcking-Str. 6-8, 66121 Saarbrücken, Deutschland / Germany
Email: info@scholars-press.com

Herstellung: siehe letzte Seite /
Printed at: see last page
ISBN: 978-3-639-76671-4

Zugl. / Approved by: National Institute of Technology Rourkela, INDIA

Abstract

Scheduling of real time tasks on cloud is one of the research problem, Where the matching of machines and completion time of the tasks are considered. Real time task's matching of machines problem is that, assume number of active hosts are p, number of VMs in each host are q. Maximum number of possible VMs to schedule a single task is $(p \times q)$. If we need to schedule r tasks, number of possibilities are $(p \times q)^r$. So scheduling of tasks is NP Hard problem.

Completion time constraint of real time task is that if task complete in dead line then only it is useful else it is not. If it is not useful then it is rejected. Earliest Dead line First(EDF) algorithm is well known algorithm for scheduling of real time tasks. EDF is Event Driven scheduling algorithm with priority assign as dynamically with respect to their deadlines. Real time tasks can be periodic, Sporadic, Aperiodic tasks. We have used Aperiodic and Periodic model to evaluate performance of varies scheduling algorithms.

In general EDF Scheduler schedule the tasks such that it assign the task to the free available machine without considering the task on that machine will meet the dead line or not. In this work checked the completion time of task on the free available machines before assigning the task to the machine. To assign the task i have used three different techniques. First Fit, Best Fit, Worst Fit. Here Fit of task means that the task will complete it's execution on that machine in it's dead line time. These three techniques and Basic EDF are used in scheduling of aperiodic tasks and also periodic tasks. We have study the perfomance of the techniques First Fit EDF(FFE), Best Fit EDF(BFE), Worst Fit EDF(WFE).

The simulation has carried out in house simulator using matlab by taking performance parameters as Guarantee Ratio(GT), VM Utilization (VU), and Through Put(TP). In simulation results it is shown that FFE, BFE and WFE algorithms are better in performance than the Basic EDF algorithm.

Contents

List of Figures

List of Tables

CHAPTER 1

Introduction

1.1 Introduction

A real time system is generally a controlling system , often embedded into
other equipment so that it is not obvious that it is even a computer. It takes in
information from its environment, processes it and generates a response. A real
time system reacts, responds and alters its actions to affect the environment in
which it is placed. A real time system implies that there is something significant
and important about its response time. A common miss-perception of a RT
system is that its response time to events should always be lightening fast. This
is not necessarily true. A Real time systems response just has to be timely, the
definition of which will vary considerably from application to application. It could
be Sec or minutes. A real time system has a guaranteed, calculated (we use the
word deterministic), worst case response time to an event under it's control.

The real time systems are those systems in which the correctness of the results of the system depends up on the logical result of computation and the time
at which the results are produced. In real time system whose correctness depends on their temporal aspects as well as their functional aspects of the results.
Performance measure of real time systems are timeliness on timing constraints
(deadlines constraints)speed/average case performance are less significant.

The schedulers give the best run time control for algorithms by using scheduling
policies. Scheduling policies compete with the real time tasks and occupy the
computational resources. By using the schedulability tests algorithms we can
test the services guarantee to meet the deadline. Schedulability tests are time

1

consuming and complicated but improves the resources in efficent manner. In the real time systems the services with a large variance of behaviours in their run times and the tests should be guarantee that the services will not miss their deadlines in all possible runs.

The general scheduling problem schedules the tasks according to the various conditions are satisfied. A task is characterized by ready time,execution time,deadline and requirement of resources. While executing the tasks, the task may be interrupted or may not be. If the task is interrupted then it is a preemptive scheduling. The tasks are having the constraints are based on the precedence relation. The execution of a task will starts after completes the execution of its predecessors tasks. The tasks are executed is characterized by the amounts of resources are available. The goals in the real time scheduling are meet the dead line,improves the utilization, reduce the context switch due to the preemption, reduce the communication cost.

Cloud computing is dynamic service provider using very large virtualized and scalable resources over the internet. Cloud computation is defined as the collection of computing and communication resources over the distributed data centres and is shared by many different users. Cloud computing has the most emerging paradigm area in the Information Technology(IT). To judge the quality of an real time applications or sevices the major criteria is time. The real time services over the internet,all the tasks will meet their deadline guarantee like hard real time systems.

1.2 Real Time Tasks Scheduling : Case Study

The Real Time Systems are becoming prevalent. The examples of real time systems in case study include Auto Mobile Application, Aircraft Control Application, Air Defense System, Computer On-Board an Aircraft, Missile Guidance System and Internet and Multimedia Applications. In a Real Time System, the correctness of the system results depends on the logical results of the computations and on the time instant at which these results are produced. The Real

Time Systems are classified based on a number of viewpoints like factors, If the factors in the computer system may be inside or outside. The special importance is placed on soft and hard real time systems.

In an **Auto Mobile Application**[9], from the brake pedal, a task may sense the pressure and the individual wheels speed, perform calculations to determine if a wheel is locked or not, if wheel is locked then activate anti lock braking actions by changing the position of the valves in the system. For instance, in the auto mobile application, if the task does not activate anti lock braking within a time interval after a wheel is locked, the vehicle is likely to enter a spin which, in turn, could result in an accident.

In an **Aircraft Control Application**[9], a task monitor the current position of the throttle, perform calculations based on the sensed position of the throttle, and based on that change the thrust of an engine by altering the fuel injected to it. These type of tasks are called as periodic tasks. A common feature of periodic tasks is that they are time critical in the sense that the system cannot work without completing them in time.

In an **Air Defense System**[9] is monitoring the incoming enemy missiles in the sky. The below example also highlights important characteristic of real time applications. Since the behavior of the controlling real time computing system must be predictable, every incoming enemy missile must be destroyed without fail. That is, it should be possible to show at design time that all the timing constraints of the application will be met as long as certain system assumptions are satisfied. By the nature of the application, the timing constraints are such that the incoming enemy missile must be destroyed within 15 sec of detection. This, in turn, imposes deadlines on other tasks which either detect, identify, engage, or launch an intercept missile. For instance, an incoming missile must be identified with 0.2 sec of detection, and if necessary, an intercept missile must be engaged within 5 sec after detection and launched within 0.5 sec of engagement. These task deadlines will in turn impose deadlines on their sub tasks, which will then impose deadline on their sub tasks, and so on.

3

Computer On Board an Aircraft: [6] The modern aircraft has the auto pilot option selected by the pilots. After selection the aircraft switches to auto pilot mode then the control of the aircraft is taken by the on board computer. The computer takes the control of take off, navigation, landing the aircraft. The computer checks the acceleration and velocity of the aircraft. The on board computer computes the X, Y and Z coordinates of the current aircraft position and compare with the prescribed track data. The system takes the necessary actions by calculatin the deviation from the track data. In this case, the system takes the sampling of data and their processing need to be completed with in a few microseconds.

Missile Guidance System: [6] In the missile guidance system the computers are placed on the missile. A guided missile has the capable of sensing or tracking the target place and home onto it. The deviation is calculated by the mounted computer and placed on the missile from the required trajectory and changes the track of the missile to guide it onto the target. The track correction tasks must be activated regularly to keep the missile on the target and the sensing of the missile should be time constraint. The tasks in the missile guidance system are required to complete within the microseconds.

Internet and Multimedia Applications:[6] The uses of the real time systems in the multimedia and Internet applications: multimedia multicast and video conferencing, the Internet router and switches. The videos are taken by the camera sand the audio signals are generated by the microphones in the video conferencing application. The sampled data has some prescribed frame rate. The frames are doing by compression and send those frames to the receiver through a network. After the frames are received by the receiver, then the receiver ordered the packets,decompressed and then played. The time constraint is at the receiver end is that the receiver takes the frames for process then play the received frames at constant rate.

4

1.3   Literature Review

In Literature Review discussion scheduling algorithms which is used in that papers are presented. Xiaomin Zhu et al.[11] In this paper,investigated the problem of energy aware scheduling for independent, aperiodic real time tasks in virtualized clouds. The scheduling objectives are to improve the system's schedulability for real-time tasks and save energy.To achieve the objectives,here employed the virtualization technique and a rolling horizon optimization scheme,and here presented a novel energy aware scheduling algorithm named EARH(Energy Aware Rolling Horizon)for real time tasks, in which a rolling horizon policy was used to enhance the systems schedulability. If this improvement apply to the any existing real time scheduling algorithms like EDF(Earliest Deadline First), RM(Rate monotonic), LLF(Least Laxity First), then this algorithms behaviours more better. Here in this paper it is applied for EDF.

Cecilia Ekelin et al.[1], In this paper,presented a non preemptive scheduling algorithm called Clairvoyant EDF(CEDF). CEDF uses a look ahead technique to determine when a task must be postponed to a later time and inserted idle times. CEDF and EDF runs with the same time complexity but CEDF is capable of scheduling 100% more task sets in many cases. It is guaranteed to schedule all task sets that EDF schedules. Jayant R. Haritsa et al.[2], In this paper, use EDF as presenting a new piority assignment algorithm called Adaptive Earliest Deadline(AED),which having character as a feedback control mechanism that detects overload conditions and modifies transaction priority assignments accordingly. Shuo Liu et al.[4],In this paper,present a utility accrued approach which account the gain by completing a real time task in time and the cost when aborting or discarding the task. This scheduling algorithm execute chooses high profitable tasks, and also the tasks are remove which lead to large penalty. This methods are applicable any Real time tasks schedulers. Here in this paper it is applied for EDF.

R.Santhosh et al.[7],This paper presents a online, preemptive scheduling with task migration algorithm for cloud computing environment is proposed in order to improve the efficiency and to minimize the response time of the tasks. If the task misses its deadline,then it will be migrated to another free virtual machine. This the maximizes the total utility of system and improves overall system performance. In simulation results the Earliest Deadline First (EDF) and proposed on is compared. Sung-Heun Oh et al.[5],In this paper, For solving the disadvantage of the LLFScheduling algorithm proposed the Modified Least Laxity First(MLLF)scheduling algorithm . MLLF scheduling algorithm defers the preemption by allowing laxity inversion as far as deadlines of tasks are not missed. Hence, MLLF scheduling algorithm perform better than LLF Scheduling algorithm.

Rashmi Sharma et al.[8],Here show the work of Task migration with EDF and RM scheduling algorithm by using Global Scheduling. For allowing migration of tasks in scheduling Global Scheduling is used. Here used two queues, a global queue is work based on RM scheduling algorithm. Local task set queue is maintaining, and the tasks are assigned to machine for execution based on EDF scheduling algorithm.

1.4   Motivation

In research direction Real time scheduling techniques can be largely divided into Dynamic and Static. Dynamic scheduling of Services can be either with static priority or dynamic priority. Examples of dynamic scheduling with static priority are 1. Rate Monotonic(RM) algorithm, 2. Deadline Monotonic(DM) algorithm. Examples of dynamic scheduling with dynamic priority are 1. Earliest Deadline First(EDF) algorithm, 2. Least laxity Time First(LLF)algorithm.

By observation, it is known that different researchers used different scheduling algorithm. Most of the researchers have been using EDF algorithm and presented some modified EDF algorithm.EDF having advantages as full processor utilization, If a set of jobs T is schedulable by any algorithm X, and then it is schedulable by EDF algorithm, In general, EDF has less context switches, throughput of EDF scheduling are great than or equal to other scheduling algorithms.

In EDF or modified EDF scheduler the tasks by following EDF, as if the VM is free on particular Host, the task having less dead line which is already arrived is assign to it. If the task completed its execution before the dead line than good . If task not completed before dead line reject the task and make VM free, which cause wastage of VM resources and results more tasks missing their dead line. So before assign the task to VMs we need to make some decision for reducing the wasting of VM resources and also number of tasks miss their deadlines.

For doing this First Fit of Finishing time in EDF algorithm(FFE), Best Fit of Finishing Time in EDF algorithms(BFE), and Worst Fit of Finishing Time in EDF algorithm(WFE) are used. These algorithms are used to check the task deadline constraint before assign the task to VM. If Task will completed it's execution before deadline in VM than only it is assigned to VM.

1.5   Problem Definition

In this thesis real time task are scheduled such that more number of tasks will meets it's deadline. Scheduling of task to free available machine is also one of the main problem. For scheduling real time tasks different types of algorithms are used. All algorithms assign task to free machine based on their constraints. EDF having Constraint as deadline of task,RM as constraint as period of task,LLF having constraint as laxity of executing tasks etc.

Now take Number of active hosts are p, number of VMs in each host are q. So maximum number of possible VMs to scheduling a single task is $(p \times q)$.If we need to schedule r tasks, number of possibilities are $(p \times q)^r$ .So scheduling of tasks is NP Hard problem.

So for matching the tasks to Host and VM in Host we need a scheduling algorithm which is in polynomial time complexity. EDF scheduling algorithm schedules the tasks as, task having deadline first schedule first. If task meets it's deadline than good else task rejected. This rejection causes wastage of resources. So my work focuses on applying Fitting method that task will meets it's deadline if it assign to VM.Initially task is rejected If task will not meet it's deadline in VM.

For this fitting process FFE,BFE and WFE are used and the objective of my work is

1.Maximize the Guarantee Ratio(GR).

2.Maximize the Utilization of VMs(UV)

3.Maximize the Through Put(TP) of task

1.6   Thesis Outline

A brief introduction of Real Time Systems ,Real time task scheduling and cloud computing,than case study,than related work ,motivation and problem statement are presented in Chapter 1. **The rest of the thesis organized in to the following chapters:**

In chapter 2, we discussed Real Time System and cloud computing: Models and Performance Metrics. In chapter 3 gives brief description of Aperiodic Task Scheduling by using Four algorithms BEDF, FFE, BFE and WFE. In chapter 4 gives brief description of Periodic Task Scheduling by using Four algorithms BEDF, FFE, BFE and WFE. chapter 5 gives brief description of Real time streaming data using MapReduce. In this chapter explanation of MapReduce, notations and model of MapReduce and finally explanation of simple example of word count is written.

Chapter 2

Real Time System and cloud computing:Models,Performance Metrics

2.1   Introduction

The theme of the thesis is to scheduling the real time tasks on providing performance parameters as Guarantee Ratio, Utilization of VMs and Through Put. We proposed the system model of the real time scheduling of tasks that will use for throughout thesis. The primary goal of the scheduling tasks in the real time systems is often to provide that the system will execute the task in such that more number of task should meet their dead lines. In a chosen time frame physically effected is the purpose of the real time systems. A real time system having two types of systems. The first one is computer called controlling system and another is environment called control system. Based on the availability of information the controlling system interacts with the environment. The real time system is differentiated from the non real time systems with a common characteristics.

- **Timing constraints** The timing constraints are impacted on the timing behaviour of the tasks in terms of its release time and absolute time or relative real deadlines of tasks. If a scheduled task will meet its timing constraints then will say that the system works correctly.

- **Safety Criticality**In the non real time systems the safety and reliability of services are independent issues, but in the many real time systems the safety and reliability are the najor issues interactively bounding together to keep it safety.

9

To maximize the utilization of resources in the cloud computing is the major concern in the Real time systems. So the tasks are mapping to the virtual machines in such way that it improves the overall performance and utilization of the system also increases. In the real time services the tasks are complete their execution before the deadlines such that the system will improves in throughput and efficiency. The system model of the RTS as shown in Fig No. 2.1 is created for the description of the system behaviour of real time distributed system with in the domain.

A real time system is generally a controlling system , often embedded into other equipment so that it is not obvious that it is even a computer. It takes in information from its environment, processes it and generates a response.

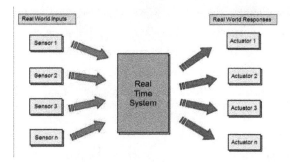

Figure 2.1: Real Time System Diagram

Cloud Computing: Cloud computing provide the computing resources to the users over the internet. The resources we needed are not keep in the hard disk of the systems, Instead of hard disk will keep the data in the virtualized resources. To access the data from the virtual resources we need the internet. Cloud services provide the software's from third party service providers and users can use this software without installing the software in their local machines. The cloud services include online file storage, web mail, social networking sites and enterprise applications. Cloud computing models can access the data from anywhere in the world. The Architecture of the cloud computing is shown in fig.2.2

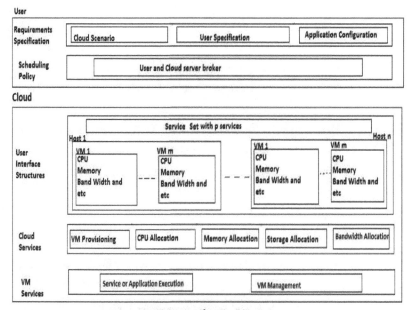

Cloud Computing Architecture

Figure 2.2: Cloud Computing Architecture

The definition of the cloud computing has been developed by the U.S. National Institute of Standards and Technology (NIST):

The cloud computing is a on demand network access to shared a computing resources like storage, servers, network and applications. The computational resources are managed by the very less effort and convenience. The cloud computing models are categorised in to three service models, four deployment models and five important characteristics.

The essential characteristics of cloud computing are resource pooling, broad network access, rapid elasticity, measured service and on-demand self service. The broad band networks will provide the over the private networks. The customers can manage their own computing resources are the on-demand self service. From the pool of resources the customers can access their own resources. The measured service is the customer can pay the bill based on their usage.

The cloud computing has three service models. The SaaS is a software as a service model describes that the user can use the software without installing the software in to their local machines. The Iaas is a infrastructure as a service provides the hard ware and computing resources. The developers will have an authority to access the resources in the IaaS. The customers develops or installs its the operating systems and application software's.The PaaS is the platform as a service provide the platform for building, testing, and creating the applications.

Cloud services are available via a private cloud, community cloud, public cloud or hybrid cloud.

The services provided by a **public cloud** are available over the internet and are owned and managed by a cloud service provider. The examples of the public cloud services like online photo storage, e-mail, social network sites. Some of the enterprise application services also provided by the public cloud.

The services provided by a **private cloud** or the cloud infrastructure is managed or operated by the solely for a specific organization. The services are managed by the organization or a third party service provider. In the community cloud, the services are shared by several organizations and the services are available only to those group of organisations. The organisations or the third party service providers owns and operates the infrastructure.

The **hybrid cloud** is a combination of any different methods of resource pooling (for example it may combination of public and community clouds).

Cloud Host The large number of systems are integrated and they act as a single machine in cloud computing technologies. The hosting solutions are depends on the single machine only but the security services are provided by many servers. The advantage of the cloud technology will integrate the resources such as ram or space and that will increase the website improvement.

A **Virtual Machine(VM)** is usually a program or operating system, which does not physically exist but is created within the another environment. A virtual machine has two components : the host and the guest. The host is the virtual machine host server , it process the memory,disk and network I/O and processing power provided by the computing resources.The independent instance of an operating system and application software are separated by the guest. In the host, virtual machine has the virtual workloads are called guests.

2.2   System model

A real time system has the computers are heterogeneously networked to resolve a single problem. So the co-ordination of activities between the computers is a complex task and deadlines makes more complex.

Definition 1   *Real Time System.* *A real time systems consists of a controlling system, a controlled system and the environment. The controlling system acquires information about the environment through input devices, performs certain computation on the data and controls output devices.*

This model is derived from the standard real time periodic task model in Liu(2000) which characterizes accurately many traditional hard real time applications, such as digital control, real time monitoring and constant bit-rate voice/video transmission etc.

The model consists of a set of n periodic tasks T = { t_1, t_2, t_3 ...... t_n }, each t_k is released periodically with a period p_k, has a deadline d_k and arrival time has a a_k . The period p_k of t_k is the minimum length of all time intervals between release times of consecutive jobs of in t_k. The size of each task $t_k \in$ T is a constant l_k. The tasks are executed on a set of heterogeneous computing system calling as Hosts H = {h_1, h_2, h_3,......, h_m}. each host h $_i$ having the VMs set as V_i={v_{i1},v_{i2},v_{i3},......,$v_{i|V_i|}$}. Each VM v_{ij} having computation power as $C(v_{ij})$.The traditional model does not capture dynamic and unpredictable environment since execution times are modelled as constants. It is inadequate for some real time systems which can having actuation tasks, action planning and one

13

or more of the tasks may contain algorithms and execution times that are affected by unpredictable environmental factors such as system load, resource failure etc. Accurate modeling of the system for performance requirement is mostly based on robust scheduling of tasks to resilient many unpredictable scenarios.

Considered each task $t_k \in T$ is represented by a tuple (a_k, p_k, l_k, d_k) where t_i is released periodically with a period of p_k and has a deadline d_k and has size as l_i and has arrival time as a_k. The perturbation environmental parameters that affect a system are modelled as $pp = [pp_1, pp_2,.., pp_n]$. Each task T_i has actual execution time e_i that is the function of environmental variable pp i.e. $e_i = f(pp)$. Generally, the basic parameter used for performance metric is utilization, given as

$$U(pp) = \sum_{r=1}^{n} \frac{e_i}{P_i} \qquad (2.2.1)$$

The system utilization U of is a function of the environmental variables. U(0) represents the portion of system utilization that is independent of environmental variables.

If taking same T set of tasks as aperiodic tasks.then considered each task $t_k \in$ T is represented by a tuple (a_k, l_k, d_k) where t_i is having deadline d_k and has size as l_i and has arrival time as a_k. Here considering only three parameters.

2.3   Workload Model

Real-time applications are normally composed of multiple tasks with different levels of criticality. A real time application usually consists of a set of co-operating tasks activated at regular interval or/and on particular events. A task typically senses the state of system, performs certain computations and if necessary sends command to change the state of system. It is very important to define the real time task. For different domains of computer science the exact meaning varies greatly. Terms such as application, task, sub task, task force and agent are used to denote the same object in some instances, and yet, have totally different meanings in others. In order to be consistent in our analysis we have chosen the following basic definition of a real-time task and a timing diagram of which has been shown in Figure No.2.3.

Definition 2 *(Real Time Task).* *A unit of computation in distributed real time system that has timing constraints. Each task associates with timing parameters like arrival time, absolute deadline, relative deadline, period over which the task is invoked again, approximate execution time and priority, which determines its importance level.*

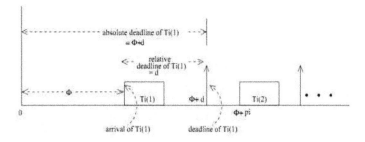

Figure 2.3: Timing Diagram of Periodic Task

The real time tasks can be modeled by parameters listed in Table 2.1. Based on the recurrence of the real time tasks, it is possible to classify them into three main categories: periodic, sporadic and aperiodic tasks.

1. **Periodic task:** Task T_i which is activated (released) regularly at fixed rate (period p_i). Normally, periodic tasks have constraints which indicate that instances of them must execute once per period p. A periodic task is represented by a tuple (Φ_i, p_i,c_i,d_i) where Φ_i is the occurrence of the instance of T_i, p_i is the period of task, c_i is the worst case execution time of T_i ,and d_i is the relative deadline of T_i. Periodic tasks can have additional parameters as shown in Table 2.2

2. **Sporadic task:** Real-time task which is activated irregularly with some known bounded rate. The bounded rate is characterized by a minimum inter-arrival period, that is, a minimum interval of time between two successive activations. The sporadic task is represented by a tuple (e_i,g_i,d_i)

15

where $e_i$is the worst case execution time, g_i denotes the minimum separation between two consecutive instances of $T_{i,}$, d_i is the relative deadline.

3. **Aperiodic task:** Real time task T_i can arise at random instants similar to sporadic task. Here the minimum separation g_i between two consecutive instances can be 0.

Application program is considered as a set of tasks i.e. $A_i = (T_{Ai,1} T_{Ai,2} \ldots T_{Ai,k})$. Each task consists of subtasks such that $T_{Ai,1} = st_1{}^{i,1}$, $st_2{}^{i,1}, \ldots st_n{}^{i,1}$. The subtasks are considered to be the correct states of a given task. Each task is mapped on a certain node of the distributed application. Hence, the resource requirement of a task

$T_i = P_{i,} \ldots P_{i+k}$ k$\in$(0,1,2,....n)

$T_i = ch_{i,} \ldots ch_{i+k}$ k$\in$(0,1,2,....m)

2.4 Concepts and Terms

2.4.1 Scheduling and Dispatching

Scheduling is the creation of a schedule: a (partially) ordered list specifying how contending accesses to one or more sequentially reusable resources will be granted. A schedule is intended to be optimal with respect to some criteria (such as timeliness ones).

Number of algorithms proposed for scheduling real time tasks, main classes of algorithms are defined as follows:

- **Preemptive.** The running task will be interrupted at any point of time after assigning the task to the processor for active any other task is called preemptive. This will be according to a predefined scheduling policy.

- **Non-preemptive.**If any task will start it execution on the proceess, it will execute until the task is completed by the processor.

- **Static.** The scheduling decisions are based on the fixed parameters before submitting the tasks to their execution.

- **Dynamic.** The scheduling decisions are based on the dynamic parameters that may change during the execution of the tasks. This will improve the resource utilization.

- **Off-line.** The scheduling algorithm executes the entire task a before their actual execution in the off-line. The schedule obtained in this way will stored in to a table and then executed by the dispatcher.

- **On-line.** The scheduling decisions are made at run time in the online scheduling algorithm. There may be a new task enters into the system or the running task terminates from execution.

- **Optimal.** An algorithm minimizes the cost function defined over the task set is called optimal algorithm. If there is no cost function defined then there is the only concern to achieve a feasible solution.

- **Heuristic.** An heuristic algorithm provides a feasible solution but it may or may not be a optimal.

In contrast, **dispatching** is the process of granting access to the currently most eligible contending entity.

2.4.2   Schedulable and Non-Schedulable Entities

Schedulable entities (e.g., threads, tasks, and processes in both the application and the system software) are scheduled by the scheduler. Non-schedulable entities are most often in the system software and can include interrupt handlers, operating system commands, packet-level network communication services, and the operating systems scheduler. Non-schedulable entities can execute continuously, periodically, or in response to events; their timeliness is a system design and implementation responsibility.

Definition 3 *Valid Schedule* *A valid schedule of a set of tasks is a schedule which satisfying the following properties:*

- *Each process can only start execution after its release time.*

- *All the precedence and resource usage constraints are satisfied.*

17

- *The total amount of processor time assigned to each task is equal to its maximum or actual execution time.*

Definition 4 *Feasible schedule A feasible schedule of a set of tasks ψ is a valid schedule by which every task completes by its deadline a set of tasks is schedulable according to a scheduling algorithm if the scheduler always produces a feasible schedule.*

Definition 5 *Optimal schedule An optimal schedule of a set of tasks ψ is valid schedule of ψ with minimal lateness. A hard real-time scheduling algorithm is optimal if the algorithm always produces a feasible schedule for a given set of tasks.*

2.4.3 Timeliness Specification

In real time systems based on timeliness specification real time tasks can be of the following type.

1. **Deadline:** A deadline is the time, in real time systems, task are acceptable only if it complete it's execution before the dead line. If task not complete it's execution then it will be rejected. Some times this rejection can cause more loss. In real time systems task may complete it's execution before deadline or may not. Some time not complete in deadline is also allowed, based on that real time systems are soft and hard.

2. **Hard Deadline** A hard real time system is one in which a failure of the system to meet the specified worst case response time to an input or real world event will lead to overall system failure. Hard real time systems are easy to spot from their specifications which talk about maximum response times and the effects of failure to meet that time. For example, a system specification might state that given input X the system will respond with output Y within 10ms. If it takes 10.1ms then the system could well fail and you are out of a job.

   Example Hard Real Time Systems: Heart Monitoring System used in Coronary Care. Engine Management, ABS, Stability and Traction Control systems in a car. Nuclear Power Station controlling the reaction. Air Traffic Control system or Auto-pilot in an aircraft or helicopter. Digital Signal Processor such as CD/MP3 player or digital filter (time is especially critical here if acceptable sound is to be produced).

In other words, failure of a hard real-time system often results in complete failure of the system, sometimes incurring significant cost and loss of life or serious injury and damage. In summary, hard real time systems are time critical.

3. **Soft Deadline** A soft real time system implies that failure to meet a specified response time merely results in system degradation not necessarily outright failure. A Soft Real time systems specification will thus quote a typical, suggested or average response time against which degradation (not necessarily failure) can be judged. The response time of a Soft Real Time system is thus not fixed and may improve or degrade within acceptable limits depending upon system loading. Of course system degradation can ultimately become system failure if the response time becomes so intolerable that it no longer functions acceptably. **Example Soft Real Time Systems** *An Elevator control system* Response time varies with the time of day and passenger load. This could be said to have failed if all the passengers decide it is quicker to walk instead, but we might consider it to work acceptably if 95% of passenger requests are met within 30 seconds, averaged over a day.*An ATM for a bank* Response time varies with the time of day and load experienced by the bank central computer. Failure could be said to have occurred if the transaction cannot be completed without annoying the customer (say 2 mins). However success might be measured by a system that on average completes 99.5% of transactions within 1 min.

RTS consists of different types of machines, networks, and interfaces to meet the requirements of widely varying application mixtures and to maximize the system performance or cost effectiveness. It is very important how to allocate resources to improve quality of service. It is the problem of mapping (matching of applications to resources and scheduling their execution).

2.4.4 Task Scheduling

The most important thing in RTS is meeting task deadlines as explained above. Scheduling of tasks involves the allocation of processors(including resources) and time to tasks in such a way that certain performance requirements are met [5]. There are several task scheduling paradigms emerge, depending on (i) whether a system performs schedulability or stability analysis, (ii) if it does, whether it is done statically or dynamically, and (iii) whether the result of the analysis itself produces a schedule according to which tasks are dispatched at run time.

2.4.5 Classification of Real-Time Task Scheduling Algorithms

Many types of classification of real time task scheduling algorithms exist. Real time systems can be classified on the basis of how they generate their responses. There are two simple classifications here

1. Event driven systems
2. Time driven systems

1.Event Driven, Real Time Systems: An event driven system, is one in which the input sensor is responsible for detecting that some important event critical to the systems success and operation has taken place or changed. The occurrence of the event thus triggers a response from the system. Events can generally be detected in one of two ways. The sensor generates an interrupt. e.g. a switch, button etc. The computer uses a polling technique to periodically interrogate the status of each sensor.

*Advantages of Interrupt Based Event Driven Systems:*More predictable, deterministic response to an event. Sensors/interrupts can be prioritised. Response time to each sensor/interrupt is independent of number of sensors (provided the system is not overloaded with interrupts or work). Importantly Use of interrupts creates spare processing power as CPU is free to do other things in between inter-rupts _Disadvantages to Interrupt Based, Event Driven Systems:_ More complex or expensive hardware. For example the system may require Sensors capable of generating an interrupt (not all can). Additional hardware to prioritise Interrupts from multiple sensors. System level code (i.e. interrupt handlers) to deal with the interrupt and trigger the execution of users code able to process it.

_Advantages of Polling in Event Driven Systems:_Easier to write. There are no asynchronous interrupts, thus there is no complex Interrupt Service Routine to be integrated into the system. The resulting polled program is single threaded. Ex-ternal Event recognition becomes synchronous to the program execution leading to systems that are more easily debugged and tested._Disadvantages of Polling in Event Driven Systems:_Sensor events can be missed, if the persist only for a brief period of time, since they may not be detected within the polling loop period. Polling Sensors makes it difficult to prioritise between them. For example there is no way for a higher priority sensor to interrupt the system when it is already dealing with a lower priority event as the CPU will be busy elsewhere and not looking for the higher priority event. Adding more sensors to a polled solution generally degrades the response time to each of them, since it takes longer to poll all the devices as part of a loop. Polling consumes lots of CPU time which means there is often no time left for the CPU to do other things.

2. TIME Driven Real-Time Systems: In such a system, the designer gen-erally decomposes the system activities into a number of smaller threads or pro-cesses (see next major topic) and ensures that the operating system scheduler runs the tasks at the prescribed time(assuming that this is possible). We will come back to this when we discuss scheduling strategies later in the course. Students should read this short article on event vs. time driven systems.

Testing Issues for Real-Time Systems: Testing real-time systems is difficult because of asynchronous real world events and hence it is almost impossible to predict what they will be doing at any one instant in time. What will an elevator be doing 5 secs after we enable it?. What will the autopilot be doing 20 mins

21

into a flight?. Testing is both expensive and time-consuming and most software systems are not exhaustively tested.It is impossible to subject the system to all combinations of inputs and timings that the system may encounter in its life. If the system should fail, it may be difficult (impossible even?) to recreate the exact same environment that existed just prior to the failure in order to figure out how and why the system failed. In fact when a RT system fails there may be nothing left of it to test.

2.5 Task Scheduling in RTS

2.5.1 Parameters and Notations

The purpose of the real time system is to execute the services with in the deadline. The scheduling of the services in the real time distributed systems can be divided into two parts. If a service wants to execute on the machine the first question is how to execute. After the task submitted to the machine once tasks have been allocated and the problem becomes each node has the feasible local schedule. The local scheduling method is equals to the scheduling method in the uniprocessor systems. The Real time task scheduling refers to the order of the services are going to execute by operating systems. The Scheduling of real-time tasks is different from ordinary task scheduling. In the general scheduling the tasks ensure fairness, prevention of deadlock and starvation but in the real time services the primary concern is the services should complete in their deadlines.

The Real time applications are like aircraft and airport,defence systems ,factories and industrialized technological infrastructure are relatively rigid requirements on their performances. The real time systems are having high degree of schedulability. So scheduling of real time services is an NP-Complete problem. To achieve the maximum throughput and resource utilization of the system based on the how we scheduled the services on the cloud system. The real time services need their computation time and communication time and data resources

SN	Parameter	Notation	Description
1	Arrival time	a_k	Time at which task arrives
2	Absolute deadline	D_k	$r_k + d_k$
3	Relative deadline	d_k	The maximum allowable job response time
4	Execution time	C_k	Time taken to complete the task
5	Maximum execution time	C_k^+	Maximum time taken to complete the task
6	Minimum execution time	C_k^-	Minimum time taken to complete the task
7	Completion time	CT_k	The instant at which a job completes execution
8	Laxity	L_i	$L_i = D_k - a_k - C_k$
9	Slack	SL_k	$L_k = SL_k \sum_{i=1}^{n} Ck$
10	Response time	RT_k	The length of time from the release time of the job to the time instant when it completes
11	Task arrival rate	λ	The rate at which tasks arrives
12	Total number of nodes	M	—
13	Release time of the task	r_k	Time at which the task is ready for processing
14	Worst case execution time	c_k	worst-case execution time of the task at each release
15	Size of task	l_k	Size of the Task in number of instructions

Table 2.1: Parameters of real time work model

to be processed in the scheduling of allocating the resources to satisfy the those transactions.

SI	Parameter	Notation	Descriptiom
1	Period of task	p_k	At all times the period and execution time of periodic tasks is known.
2	Phase of the task	Φ_k	$\Phi_k = r_{k,1}$ $(J_{k,1})$the release time of the first J_k in T_k
3	Utilization	u_k	$u_k = e_k \, / \, p_k$
4	Total utilization	U	$U = \sum_{i=1}^{n} u_k$
5	Hyperperiod	H	The least common multiple of p_k for k=1, 2,...,n

Table 2.2: Periodic task parameters

2.5.2 scheduling model

The scheduling model used in my complete thesis is shown in Fig No. 2.4, it having components as Users, Ready Queue which is global for all, Scheduler which schedules the task, Host, VMs, Local queue for each VMs.

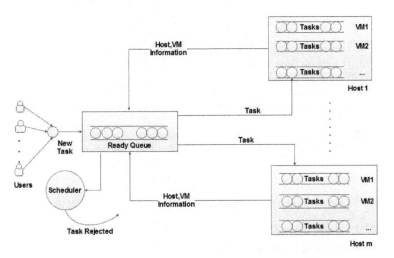

Figure 2.4: Scheduling Diagram

2.5.3   Assumptions on Scheduling Tasks

1. System has any number of finite VMs running on each host to provide task.

2. A VM can have finite queue to store the executing tasks.

3. Scheduling decision has been manage by a central scheduler.

4. Scheduling is non-preemptive.

5. The tasks, which are miss deadline are rejected.

6. The Ready queue holds both new task and waiting task to be executed.

7. A scheduling process is triggered by new task, and all the task in the ready queue will be rescheduled.

2.5.4   Task execution States

Here in Fig No. 2.5 show the state which is followed by task in it's execution.

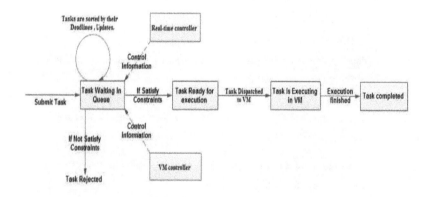

Figure 2.5: Task Execution States

2.5.5   Scheduling Steps

Step1: Arriving of new task in to ready queue that new task is stored in ready queue.

Step2: Scheduler checks the hosts, VMs and task execution information and updated it.

Step3: The tasks in Ready Queue are sorted according to their deadlines to facilitate the scheduling operation

Step4: When a task in the Ready queue is ready to execute, the task is dispatched to assigned Host and VM in that host.

Step5: If task on VM completed its execution,than make VM free

2.6 Performance Metrics

There are number of system performance measures like reliability, availability, and throughput are some of suitable parameters for real time computers.

1. **Guarantee Ratio(GR):** it is defined as the ratio between the number of tasks meets their respective deadline to total number of tasks, that is

   Guarantee Ratio=(number of tasks meets their respective deadline)/(total number of tasks)

2. **Utilization of VMs(UV):** It is defined as the the amount of useful work done by VMs in it's life time, useful work means task executed on VM must meets it's deadline, that is

   Utilization of VMs=(Σsize of tasks meets deadline, ∀task ε Task set)/(Σcomputation power of VMs in each Host, ∀Host ε Host set and VM ε VM set)

3. **Through Put(TP):** It is defined as the number of tasks meets their dead lines successfully, that is

   Through Put=Number of tasks meets their dead line

4. **Makespan(M):** The total execution time of application.

5. **Slack of task(S) :** A time window within which the task can be delayed without affecting the makespan.

6. **Entropy of schedule:** It is based on the probability of an execution path that will become critical.

7. **Expected makespan(E(M)):**The average value of the makespan.

In this thesis work Guarantee Ratio, Utilization of VMs and Through Put are used as performance metrics for scheduling tasks.

2.7 Conclusion

In this chapter, we discussed real time system model, workload model, scheduling model, scheduling steps and other issues related to the real time task scheduling and also discussed about performance parameters in scheduling of real time tasks.

CHAPTER **3**

Aperiodic Task Scheduling

3.1 Introduction

Aperiodic Task are set of task which are having single instant. Aperiodic tasks which are activated at unforeseen times, e.g. button click. The scheduling problem for aperiodic tasks is very different from the scheduling problem for periodic tasks. Scheduling algorithms for aperiodic tasks must be able to guarantee the deadlines for hard deadline aperiodic tasks and provide good average response times for soft deadline aperiodic tasks even though the occurrences of the aperiodic requests are non deterministic. The aperiodic scheduling algorithm must also accomplish these goals without compromising the hard deadlines of the periodic tasks.

An aperiodic task is in many ways similar to a sporadic task. An aperiodic task can arise at random instants. However, in case of an aperiodic task, the minimum separation between two consecutive instances can be 0. That is, two or more instances of an aperiodic task might occur at the same time instant. Also, the deadline for an aperiodic tasks is expressed as either an average value or is expressed statistically. Aperiodic tasks are generally soft real-time tasks.It is easy to realize why aperiodic tasks need to be soft real-time tasks.Aperiodic tasks can recur in quick succession. It therefore becomes very difficult to meet the deadlines of all instances of an aperiodic task. When several aperiodic tasks recur in a quick succession, there is a bunching of the task instances and it might lead to a few deadline misses.

3.2   Aperiodic Task scheduling model

SI	Notation	Description
1	H	Host set.
2	H_a	Active Host set.
3	h_i	i^{th} Host.
4	V_i	i^{th} Host VM set.
5	v_{ij}	i^{th} Host j^{th} VM.
6	$C(v_{ij})$	i^{th} Host j^{th} VM Computation Power.
7	T	Task set.
8	t_k	k^{th} task in set T.
9	a_k	k^{th} task arrival time.
10	l_k	k^{th} task size.
11	d_k	k^{th} task deadline.
12	st_{ijk}	start time of Task t_k on VM v_{ij}.
13	et_{ijk}	execution time of Task t_k on VM v_{ij}.
14	ft_{ijk}	finishing time of Task t_k on VM v_{ij}.
15	S	Set of Task meets its Deadline successfully.
16	s_l	l^{th} task in set S.
17	$|S|/|T|$	Guarantee Ratio(GR).
18	$|S|$	Through Put(TP).

Table 3.1: Aperiodic tasks scheduling parameters

Here target a virtualized cloud that is characterized by an infinite set $H = \{h_1, h_2, h_3, ...\}$ of physical computing hosts providing the hardware infrastructure for creating virtualized resources to satisfy users requirements. The active host set is modelled by H_a with n elements as $H_a = \{h_1, h_2, h_3, ..., h_n\}; H_a \subseteq H$. For a given host h_i it is characterized by its CPU performance defined by Million Instructions Per Second (MIPS). For each host h_i it contains a set of virtual machines (VMs) as $V_i = \{v_{i1}, v_{i2}, v_{i3}, ..., v_{im}\}; m = |V_i|$ For each VM v_{ij} , having CPU performance as $C(v_{ij})$,Here It is in number of instructions per second . Hosts and VMs in each host are generated dynamically[11].

Now consider a set $T = \{t_1, t_2, t_3, ...\}$ of independent tasks that arrive dynamically. The task t_k having parameters as $t_k = \{a_k, l_k, d_k\}$ Where, a_k is arrival time, l_k is Service length/size and d_k is deadline time.

Let st_{ijk} be the start time of Task t_k on VM v_{ij} ,et_{ijk} be the execution time of task t_k on VM v_{ij} and ft_{ijk} is the finish time of task t_k on VM v_{ij}.[11]

$$et_{ijk} = l_k/C(v_{ij}) \tag{1}$$

$$ft_{ijk} = st_{ijk} + et_{ijk} \tag{2}$$

Assume set of Task meets its Deadline denoted by S and S is sub set of T, this S is stated below

$$S = \{s_1, s_2, s_3, ..., s_o\}; o = |S|; S \subseteq T \tag{3}$$

here s_l is task which belongs to T as well as S and having same parameters that t_k having.So

$$ft_{ijl} \leq d_l; \forall s_l \in S \tag{4}$$

The objective of this work is to schedule the newly arriving task t_k among the hosts VMs to maximize the Guarantee Ratio(GR) ,Maximizes the Utilization of VMs(UV), and maximizes the Through Put(TP) set of tasks in S represented by

$MAX\{|S|/|T|\}$ (5)

MAX\{Utilization of VMs(UV)\}   (6)

$MAX\{|S|\}$ (7)

3.3   Scheduling Algorithms

3.3.1   Algorithms Pseudo Code

This section having discussion of the four algorithms Basic EDF(BEDF), First Fit EDF(FFE), Best Fit EDF(BFE) and Worst Fit EDF(WFE).In that Basic EDF(BEDF) is the existing algorithm and next three First Fit EDF(FFE), Best Fit EDF(BFE) and Worst Fit EDF(WFE) are the proposed algorithm.

Here Inputs are T:Set of n Tasks, H:Set of m active Hosts, V_i:Set of VMs on Host H_i, C:Computation power matrix of m hosts with their VMs and Output is Executed Task Set $ETS_{i,j}$ Having tasks, which are successfully meet their deadlines on VM j on Host i

In the basic EDF algorithm, Algorithm3.3.1.1, the scheduler checks the free available VM and directly assigns the task to the VM. In this BEDF scheduler does not check the constraint that task will meet its dead line or not. So few tasks will miss their deadline, and utilization of resources are also reduced.

In FFE algorithm scheduler, Algorithm3.3.1.2, if VM is available freely to assign a task then the scheduler checks the constraint that the task will meet its deadline constraint or not. If not meet its constraint then the scheduler checks with the next available free VMs. After checking the all free VMs, If the task is not assigned to any VM then the scheduler checks again that if any VM free after completion of its execution, This process will continues till the task reaches its dead line.

Algorithm 1 Basic EDF

Input: T, H, V_i:Set of VMs on Host H_i

Output: ETS:Successfully Executed Task Matrix

1: MAX=max$\{d_k, \forall t_k \epsilon T\}$

2: **for** $i \leftarrow 1$ to MAX **do**

3:     RQ is empty set //Ready Queue

4:     **for** j$\leftarrow 1$ to No.of Tasks **do**

5:         **if** $(a_j \leq i$ AND t_j not assign) **then**

6:             $RQ \leftarrow RQ \cup t_j$

7:         **end if**

8:     **end for**

9:     Sort RQ as Ascending order of Dead line of Tasks

10:     **for** $m \leftarrow 1$ to length(RQ) **do**

11:         **for** $k \leftarrow 1$ to No.of Hosts **do**

12:             **for** $l \leftarrow 1$ to No.of VMs in Host(k) **do**

13:                 **if** $VM_{k,l}$ is free **then**

14:                     Assign Task RQ_m to $VM_{k,l}$

15:                 **end if**

16:             **end for**

17:         **end for**

18:     **end for**

19:     **for** $k \leftarrow 1$ to No.of Hosts **do**

20:         **for** $l \leftarrow 1$ to No.of VMs in Host(k) **do**

21:             **if** Task on $VM_{k,l}$ complete execution **then**

22:                 $ETS_{k,l} \leftarrow$ (Executed Task on $VM_{k,l}$)

23:                 Free $VM_{k,l}$

24:             **end if**

25:             **if** Task on $VM_{k,l}$ reach dead line **then**

26:                 Free $VM_{k,l}$

27:             **end if**

28:         **end for**

29:     **end for**

30: **end for**

Algorithm 2 First Fit EDF

Input: T, H, V_i:Set of VMs on Host H_i

Output: ETS:Successfully Executed Task Matrix

 1: MAX=max$\{d_k, \forall t_k \epsilon T\}$

 2: **for** $i \leftarrow 1$ to MAX **do**

 3:    RQ is empty set //Ready Queue

 4:    **for** j$\leftarrow$1 to No.of Tasks **do**

 5:       **if** $(a_j \leq i$ AND t_j not assign) **then**

 6:          $RQ \leftarrow RQ \cup t_j$

 7:       **end if**

 8:    **end for**

 9:    Sort RQ as Ascending order of Dead line of Tasks

10:    **for** $m \leftarrow 1$ to length(RQ) **do**

11:       **for** $k \leftarrow 1$ to No.of Hosts **do**

12:          **for** $l \leftarrow 1$ to No.of VMs in Host(k) **do**

13:             **if** $VM_{k,l}$ is free AND $ft_{m,k,l} \leq d_m$ **then**

14:                Assign Task RQ_m to $VM_{k,l}$

15:             **end if**

16:          **end for**

17:       **end for**

18:    **end for**

19:    **for** $k \leftarrow 1$ to No.of Hosts **do**

20:       **for** $l \leftarrow 1$ to No.of VMs in Host(k) **do**

21:          **if** Task on $VM_{k,l}$ complete execution **then**

22:             $ETS_{k,l} \leftarrow$ (Executed Task on $VM_{k,l}$)

23:             Free $VM_{k,l}$

24:          **end if**

25:       **end for**

26:    **end for**

27: **end for**

Algorithm 3 BestFitEDF

Input: T, H, V_i:Set of VMs on Host H_i

Output: ETS:Successfully Executed Task Matrix

1: MAX=max$\{d_k, \forall t_k \epsilon T\}$

2: **for** $i \leftarrow 1$ to MAX **do**

3:      RQ is empty set //Ready Queue

4:      **for** j$\leftarrow$1 to No.of Tasks **do**

5:         **if** $(a_j \leq i$ AND t_j not assign) **then**

6:            $RQ \leftarrow RQ \cup t_j$

7:         **end if**

8:      **end for**

9:      Sort RQ as Ascending order of Dead line of Tasks

10:      **for** $m \leftarrow 1$ to length(RQ) **do**

11:         FT is empty set

12:         **for** $k \leftarrow 1$ to No.of Hosts **do**

13:            **for** $l \leftarrow 1$ to No.of VMs in Host(k) **do**

14:               **if** $VM_{k,l}$ is free AND $ft_{m,k,l} \leq d_m$ **then**

15:                 FT $\leftarrow$ FT $\cup ft_{m,k,l}$

16:               **end if**

17:            **end for**

18:         **end for**

19:         Assign Task RQ_m to $VM_{k,l}$ such that $ft_{m,k,l}$=min$\{$FT$\}$

20:      **end for**

21:      **for** $k \leftarrow 1$ to No.of Hosts **do**

22:         **for** $l \leftarrow 1$ to No.of VMs in Host(k) **do**

23:            **if** Task on $VM_{k,l}$ complete execution **then**

24:               $ETS_{k,l} \leftarrow$ (Executed Task on $VM_{k,l}$)

25:               Free $VM_{k,l}$

26:            **end if**

27:         **end for**

28:      **end for**

29: **end for**

34

In BFE algorithm scheduler, Algorithm3.3.1.3, if VMs are available freely to assign a task then the scheduler checks the constraint that the task will meets its deadline constraint or not with all the free VMs. Among the constraint satisfied VMs set, the scheduler selects the VM has the minimum finishing time, and the task assigns to that VM. If the task does not meet the constraint on any VM then the scheduler checks again that if any VM free after completion of its execution, This process will continues till the task reaches its dead line.

In WFE algorithm scheduler, Algorithm3.3.1.4, if VMs are available freely to assign a task then the scheduler checks the constraint that the task will meets its deadline constraint or not with all the free VMs. Among the constraint satisfied VMs set, the scheduler selects the VM has the maximum finishing time, and the task assigns to that VM. If the task does not meet the constraint on any VM then the scheduler checks again that if any VM free after completion of its execution, This process will continues till the task reaches its dead line.

Algorithm 4 Worst Fit EDF

Input: T, H, V_i:Set of VMs on Host H_i

Output: ETS:Successfully Executed Task Matrix

1: MAX=max$\{d_k, \forall t_k \epsilon T\}$

2: **for** $i \leftarrow 1$ to MAX **do**

3:     RQ is empty set //Ready Queue

4:     **for** j$\leftarrow 1$ to No.of Tasks **do**

5:        **if** $(a_j \leq i$ AND t_j not assign) **then**

6:           $RQ \leftarrow RQ \cup t_j$

7:        **end if**

8:     **end for**

9:     Sort RQ as Ascending order of Dead line of Tasks

10:     **for** $m \leftarrow 1$ to length(RQ) **do**

11:        FT is empty set

12:        **for** $k \leftarrow 1$ to No.of Hosts **do**

13:           **for** $l \leftarrow 1$ to No.of VMs in Host(k) **do**

14:              **if** $VM_{k,l}$ is free AND $ft_{m,k,l} \leq d_m$ **then**

15:                 FT $\leftarrow$ FT $\cup ft_{m,k,l}$

16:              **end if**

17:           **end for**

18:        **end for**

19:        Assign Task RQ_m to $VM_{k,l}$ such that $ft_{m,k,l}$=max$\{$FT$\}$

20:     **end for**

21:     **for** $k \leftarrow 1$ to No.of Hosts **do**

22:        **for** $l \leftarrow 1$ to No.of VMs in Host(k) **do**

23:           **if** Task on $VM_{k,l}$ complete execution **then**

24:              $ETS_{k,l} \leftarrow$ (Executed Task on $VM_{k,l}$)

25:              Free $VM_{k,l}$

26:           **end if**

27:        **end for**

28:     **end for**

29: **end for**

3.3.2   Time complexity of four algorithms

Assume d_{max} be the maximum dead line of all dead lines of task set T,n be the number of active available host,m be the maximum possible VMs in any host,finally p be the maximum number of tasks that can be present in Ready Queue in time span between 1 to d_{max}.

Now time complexity of algorithm to complete is

$$d_{max} \times (p\log(p) + p \times n \times m + n \times m)$$

where d_{max} is the time span of scheduling, it is multiply by three parts, in that $p\log(p) + p$ is multiply because sorting of ready queue ,here maximum possible task at any time is p, multiplication with $p \times n \times m$ is done because assign of tasks in ready queue to host's VM, multiplication with $n \times m$ is done because free the VMs in each host after complete the execution of task.

Now finally we get

$$d_{max} \times (p\log(p) + p \times n \times m + n \times m) = O(d_{max} \times p \times n \times m)$$

So time complexity of four algorithms is $O(d_{max} \times p \times n \times m)$

3.4   Simulation

Here discussion of the Simulation Model, Simulation Assumptions, simulation Results and explanation about results are present.

3.4.1   Simulation Model

The simulation of algorithms is done in house simulator using MATLAB R2009a is used and used simulation model sequence diagram is shown below.

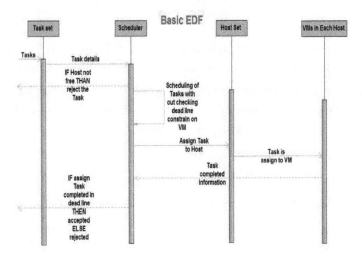

Figure 3.1: EDF scheduler model sequence

In fig3.1, it is shown by the sequence as steps of the simulation work in case of Basic EDF. In diagram it is shown that the scheduler assign task to free available Host's VM with out check deadline constrain.

In fig3.2, it is shown by the sequence as steps of the simulation work in case of modified EDF, they are FFE, BFE and WFE. In diagram it is shown that the scheduler assign task to free available Host's VM with check deadline constrain.

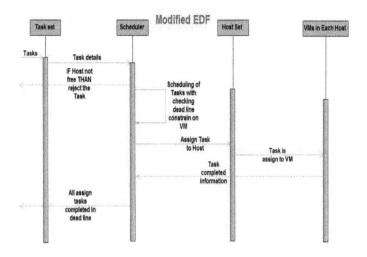

Figure 3.2: Modified EDF scheduler model sequence

3.4.2 Simulation Assumptions and Performance Parameters

Assumptions of Task, Host ,VM parameters in the simulation model

Task

1. Number of Task in sequence $\{2, 4, 6, ..., 50\}$.

2. Arrival Time of Tasks in Range(CC) [1,10].

3. Size of Tasks in Range(NIs) (0,10000].

4. Dead line of Tasks in Range(CC) (1,20].

5. All are Randomly Generated in mention Range.

Host and VMs

1. Number of Hosts are 3.

2. Number of VMs in each Host in Range [2 20].

3. Computation Power of VMs in Range(NIPC) (0,5000].

4. All are Randomly Generated in mention Range.

Performance parameters used in this simulation are

1. Guarantee Ratio(GR).

2. Utilization of VMs(UV).

3. Through Put(TP).

   Here Guarantee ratio(GR), Utilization of VMs(UV) and Through Put(TP) is calculated by varying number of task by taking Host and VMs as fixed in number, and also varying number of VMs in each Host by taking Task as fixed in number.

3.4.3 Simulation Results

In Simulation Results Graph is drawn between sets {GT, UV, TP}, {Number of Tasks, Number of VMs}, After that explanation of that graphs is done.

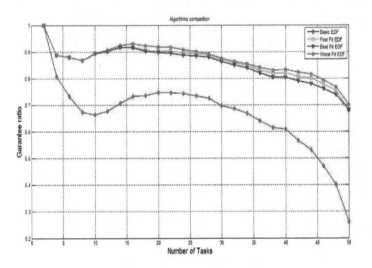

Figure 3.3: Guarantee Ratio Vs Number of Tasks

   The fig3.3 is plotted between Guarantee Ration and Number of Tasks, The fig3.5 is plotted between Utilization of VMs and Number of Tasks, The fig3.7 is plotted between Through Put and Number of Tasks, and it shows the behaviour of the four algorithms BEDF, FFE, BFE and WFE by draw graph . Here the number of Host and VMs are fixed, and varying the number of tasks. It is observed that the three proposed algorithm are better than the Basic EDF. As number of

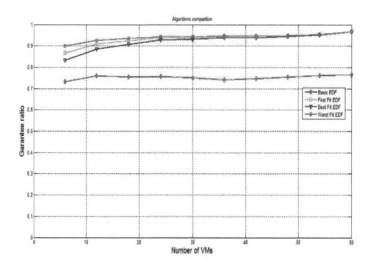

Figure 3.4: Guarantee Ratio Vs Number of VMs

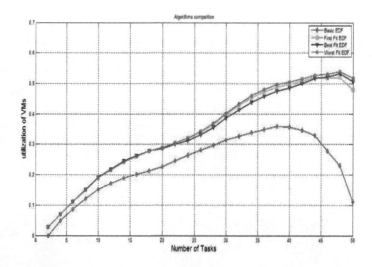

Figure 3.5: Utilization of VMs Vs Number of Tasks

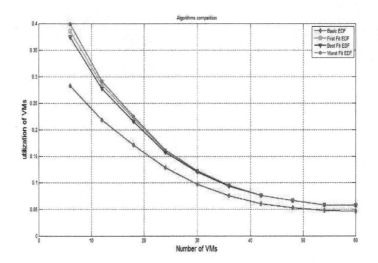

Figure 3.6: Utilization of VMs Vs Number of VMs

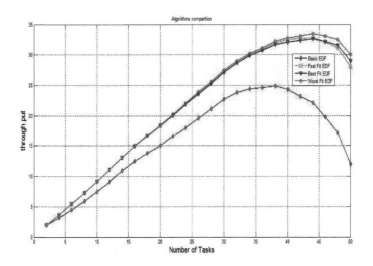

Figure 3.7: Through Put Vs Number of Tasks

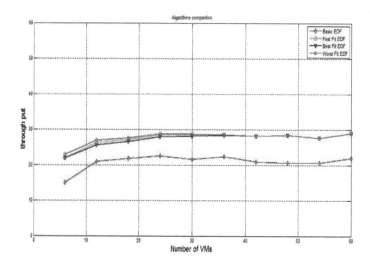

Figure 3.8: Through Put Vs Number VMs

tasks are increases the three proposed algorithms performance increases then Basic EDF.

Fig3.4 shows the behaviour of the four algorithms BEDF, FFE, BFE and WFE by drawing graph between Guarantee Ratio and Number of VMs, Fig3.6 shows the graph between Utilization of VMs and Number of VMs, Fig3.8 shows the graph between Through Put and Number of VMs.. Here the number of Host, Tasks are fixed and varying the number of VMs. It is observed that the three proposed algorithm are better performed than the Basic EDF. As number of VMs are increases the three proposed algorithms performance increases then Basic EDF.

3.5 Conclusion

In this chapter we have seen that Aperiodic tasks are scheduling by four scheduling algorithms BEDF, FFE, BFE and WFE. By simulation results it is shown that the three proposed algorithms always behaves better than that of Basic EDF in different performance parameter consideration.

43

CHAPTER 4

Periodic Task Scheduling

=====

4.1 Introduction

A periodic task is one that repeats after a certain fixed time interval. The precise time instants at which periodic tasks recur are usually demarcated by clock interrupts.For this reason, periodic tasks are sometimes referred to as clock-driven tasks.The fixed time interval after which a task repeats is called the period of the task.A vast majority of the tasks present in a typical real-time system are periodic.The reason for this is that many activities carried out by real-time systems are periodic in nature, for example monitoring certain conditions, polling information from sensors at regular intervals to carry out certain action at regular intervals (such as drive some actuators).

We shall consider examples of such tasks found in a typical chemical plant.In a chemical plant several temperature monitors, pressure monitors, and chemical concentration monitors periodically sample the current temperature, pressure, and chemical concentration values which are then communicated to the plant controller.The instances of the temperature, pressure, and chemical concentration monitoring tasks normally get generated through the interrupts received from a periodic timer.These inputs are used to compute corrective actions required to maintain the chemical reaction at a certain rate. The corrective actions are then carried out through actuators.

4.2 Periodic Task scheduling model

SI	Notation	Description
1	H	Host set.
2	H_a	Active Host set.
3	h_i	i^{th} Host.
4	V_i	i^{th} Host VM set.
5	v_{ij}	i^{th} Host j^{th} VM.
6	$C(v_{ij})$	i^{th} Host j^{th} VM Computation Power.
7	T	Task set.
8	t_k	k^{th} task in set T.
9	a_k	k^{th} task arrival times set.
10	l_k	k^{th} task size set.
11	p_k	k^{th} task period set.
12	d_k	k^{th} task deadline set.
13	r_{kl}	k^{th} task ready time at l^{th} instant .
14	d_{kl}	k^{th} task dead line at l^{th} instant .
15	st_{ijkl}	start time of Task t_k with l^{th} instant on VM v_{ij}.
16	et_{ijkl}	execution time of Task t_k with l^{th} instant on VM v_{ij}.
17	ft_{ijkl}	finishing time of Task t_k with l^{th} instant on VM v_{ij}.
18	S	Set of Task meets its Deadline successfully.
19	s_l	l^{th} task in set S.
20	$|S|/|T|$	Guarantee Ratio(GR).
21	$|S|$	Through Put(TP).

Table 4.1: Periodic tasks scheduling parameters

Here target a virtualized cloud that is characterized by an infinite set $H = \{h_1, h_2, h_3, ...\}$ of physical computing hosts providing the hardware infrastructure for creating virtualized resources to satisfy user's requirements. The active host set is modelled by H_a with n elements as $H_a = \{h_1, h_2, h_3, ..., h_n\}; H_a \subseteq H$. For a given host h_i it is characterized by its CPU performance defined by Million Instructions Per Second (MIPS). For each host h_i it contains a set of virtual machines (VMs) as $V_i = \{v_{i1}, v_{i2}, v_{i3}, ..., v_{im}\}; m = |V_i|$ For each VM v_{ij} , having CPU performance as $C(v_{ij})$,Here It is in number of instructions per second . Hosts and VMs in each host are generated dynamically.[11]

Here consider a set $T = \{t_1, t_2, t_3, ...\}$ of independent tasks that arrive dynamically. The task t_k having parameters as $t_k = \{a_k, l_k, d_k, p_k\}$ Where, a_k is arrival time, l_k is Service length/size and d_k is deadline time.p_k is period of task. For periodic task all parameter are represented as sets. The elements in set defined as

Now take r_k as ready time of task, than the ready time set for instance of tasks t_k defined as $r_k = \{r_{k1}, r_{k2}, r_{k3}, ..., r_{k|r_k|}\}$
where $r_{kl} = (l-1) \times p_k$ if $l \neq 1$ and $r_{kl} = r_k$ if $l == 1$

l_{kl} is same as l_k for all instants l

$d_k = \{d_{k1}, d_{k2}, d_{k3}, ..., d_{k|d_k|}\}$
where $d_{kl} = l \times d_k$ for all instants l

p_{kl} is same as p_k for all instants l

Let st_{ijkl} be the start time of Task t_k with instant l on VM v_{ij} ,et_{ijkl} be the execution time of task t_k with instant l on VM v_{ij} and ft_{ijkl} is the finish time of task t_k with instant l on VM v_{ij} .

$$et_{ijkl} = l_{kl}/C(v_{ij}) \tag{1}$$

$$ft_{ijkl} = st_{ijkl} + et_{ijkl} \tag{2}$$

Assume set of Task meets its Deadline denoted by S and S is sub set of T, this S is stated below

$$S = \{s_1, s_2, s_3, ..., s_{|S|}\}; S \subseteq T \tag{3}$$

here s_k is task which belongs to T as well as S and having same parameters that t_k having.So

$$ft_{ijkl} \leq d_{kl}; \forall s_k \in S \text{ ; for all instants of } s_k \tag{4}$$

The objective of this work is to schedule the newly arriving task t_k among the hosts VMs to maximize the Guarantee Ratio(GR) ,Maximizes the Utilization of VMs(UV), and maximizes the Through Put(TP) set of tasks in S represented by

$$MAX\{|S|/|T|\} \tag{5}$$

$$MAX\{\text{Utilization of VMs(UV)}\} \tag{6}$$

$$MAX\{|S|\} \tag{7}$$

4.3   Scheduling Algorithms

4.3.1   Algorithms Pseudo Code

This section having discussion of the four algorithms Basic EDF(BEDF), First Fit EDF(FFE), Best Fit EDF(BFE) and Worst Fit EDF(WFE).In Chapter3 algorithms for Aperiodic Tasks are written. If we want to apply it to Periodic task add this periodic tasks generation algorithm Algorithm 4.3.1.

4.3.2   Time complexity of algorithms

The complexity of scheduling algorithm is same as algorithms discuss in chapter3. The algorithm 4.3.1 is added as internal step to that algorithms. But parameters definition changed. Assume d_{max} be the LCM of all dead lines of task set T,n be the number of active available host,m be the maximum possible VMs in any

---

Algorithm 5 periodic tasks generation algorithm

Input: T:Set of n Tasks with parameters.

Output: T:Set of n periodic Tasks.

1: $t_k.instant \leftarrow 1 \ \forall t_k \in T$

2: MAX=LCM$\{p_k, \forall t_k \epsilon T\}$

3: **for** $i \leftarrow 1$ to MAX **do**

4:     **for** $j \leftarrow 1$ to No.of Tasks **do**

5:         **if** $(i == d_j$ OR execution completed) **then**

6:             $a_j \leftarrow (t_j.instant * p_j)$

7:             $d_j \leftarrow (t_j.instant + 1) * d_j$

8:             $t_j.instant \leftarrow t_j.instant + 1$

9:         **end if**

10:     **end for**

11: **end for**

---

host,finally p be the maximum number of tasks that can be present in Ready Queue in time span between 1 to d_{max}.

Now time complexity of algorithm to complete is

$$d_{max} \times (p\log(p) + p \times n \times m + n \times m)$$

where d_{max} is the time span of scheduling, it is multiply by three parts, in that $p\log(p) + p$ is multiply because sorting of ready queue ,here maximum possible task at any time is p, multiplication with $p \times n \times m$ is done because assign of tasks in ready queue to host's VM, multiplication with $n \times m$ is done because free the VMs in each host after complete the execution of task and parameters of task on VM is updated.

Now finally we get

$$d_{max} \times (p\log(p) + p \times n \times m + n \times m) = O(d_{max} \times p \times n \times m)$$

So time complexity of four algorithms is $O(d_{max} \times p \times n \times m)$

4.4 Simulation

4.4.1 Simulation Model

The simulation of algorithms is done in house simulator using MATLAB R2009a is used and used simulation model sequence diagram is shown in chapter 3.

In fig3.1 it is shown the by sequence that steps of my simulation work in case of Basic EDF. In fig3.2 it is shown the by sequence that steps of my simulation work in case of modified EDF, they are FFE, BFE and WFE.

4.4.2 Simulation Assumptions and Performance Parameters

Assumptions of Task, Host ,VM parameters in the simulation model

Task

1. Number of Task in sequence $\{2, 4, 6, ..., 20\}$.
2. Arrival Time of Tasks in Range(CC) [1,5].
3. Size of Tasks in Range(NIs) (0,10000].
4. Dead line of Tasks in Range(CC) (1,10].
5. All are Randomly Generated in mention Range.

Host and VMs

1. Number of Hosts are 5.
2. Number of VMs in each Host [2 10].
3. Computation Power of VMs in Range(NIPC) (0,7500].
4. All are Randomly Generated in mention Range.

Performance parameters used in this simulation are

1. Guarantee Ratio(GR).
2. Utilization of VMs(UV).
3. Through Put(TP).

Here Guarantee ratio(GR), Utilization of VMs(UV) and Through Put(TP) is calculated by varying number of task by taking Host and VMs as fixed in number, and also varying number of VMs in each Host by taking Task as fixed in number.

4.4.3 Simulation Results

In Simulation Results Graph is drawn between sets {GT, UV, TP},{Number of Tasks,Number of VMs}, so totally six graphs are shown. After that explanation of that graphs is done.

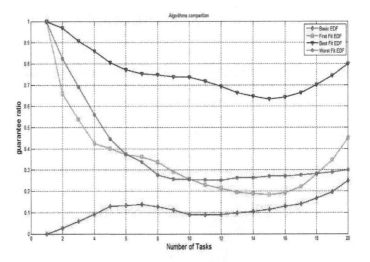

Figure 4.1: Guarantee Ratio Vs Number of Tasks

The fig3.3 is plotted between Guarantee Ration and Number of Tasks, The fig3.5 is plotted between Utilization of VMs and Number of Tasks, The fig3.7 is plotted between Through Put and Number of Tasks, and it shows the behaviour of the four algorithms BEDF, FFE, BFE and WFE by draw graph . Here the number of Host and VMs are fixed, and varying the number of tasks. It is observed that the three proposed algorithm are better than the Basic EDF. As number of tasks are increases the three proposed algorithms performance increases then

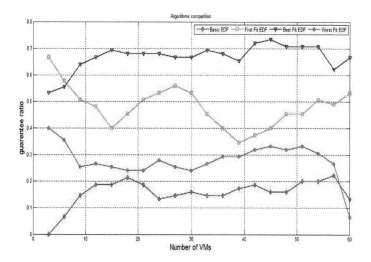

Figure 4.2: Guarantee Ratio Vs Number of VMs

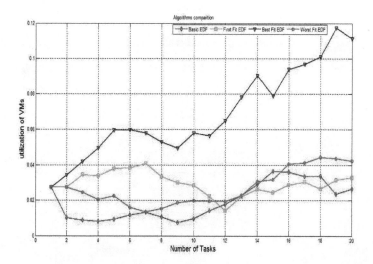

Figure 4.3: Utilization of VMs Vs Number of Tasks

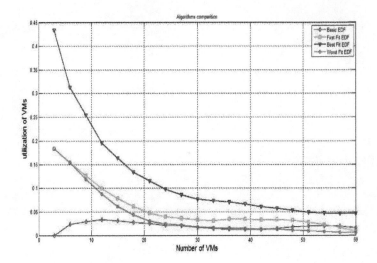

Figure 4.4: Utilization of VMs Vs Number of VMs

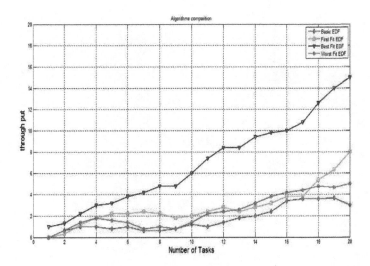

Figure 4.5: Through Put Vs Number of Tasks

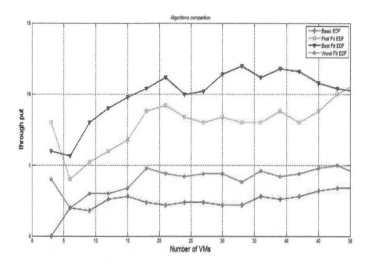

Figure 4.6: Through Put Vs Number VMs

Basic EDF.

Fig3.4 shows the behaviour of the four algorithms BEDF, FFE, BFE and WFE
by drawing graph between Guarantee Ratio and Number of VMs, Fig3.6 shows the
graph between Utilization of VMs and Number of VMs, Fig3.8 shows the graph
between Through Put and Number of VMs.. Here the number of Host, Tasks
are fixed and varying the number of VMs. It is observed that the three proposed
algorithm are better performed than the Basic EDF. As number of VMs are
increases the three proposed algorithms performance increases then Basic EDF.

4.5   Conclusion

In this chapter we have seen that Periodic tasks are scheduling by four scheduling
algorithms BEDF, FFE, BFE and WFE. By simulation results it is shown that
the three proposed algorithms always behaves better than that of Basic EDF in
different performance parameter consideration.

CHAPTER 5

Real time streaming data using MapReduce

5.1 Introduction

The term of Big Data has been coined referring to those challenges and advantages derived from collecting and processing vast amounts of data. Big Data is about the insight that we want to extract from information. There are many well known applications that are based on Cloud Computing such as email servers(Gmail), social media(Twitter), or storage sharing and backup(Dropbox). All this software manage high volumes of data, where fast responses are essential, and with information coming at a high rate in a semi-structured or unstructured way. Cloud Computing is an environment based on using and providing services. Cloud Computing offers scalability with respect to the use of resources, low administration effort, flexibility in the pricing model and mobility for the software user. Under these assumptions, it is obvious that the Cloud Computing paradigm benefits large projects, such as the ones related with Big Data.

MapReduce, a popular programming model for processing data intensive tasks, has achieved great success in a wide range of applications such as search indexing, social network mining, collaborative recommendation, and spam detection. MapReduce is a programming model Google has used successfully is processing its big data sets However, the ability of MapReduce is limited in two respects by its default schedulers. First, it does not support concurrent services sharing a cloud data center and second, it fails to guarantee response time for deadline constrained services. The MapReduce Architecture provides Automatic parallelism and distribution, Fault tolerance, I/O scheduling, Monitoring and status updates. MapReduce is the Programming model from LISP and other functional languages. Word counting is the one of the application of MapReduce using Hadoop method.

Characteristics of Mapreduce, Very large scale data is used peta, exa bytes. Write once and read many data allows for parallelism without mutexes, Map and Reduce are the main operations are simple code. There are other supporting operations such as combine and partition. All the map should be completed before reduce operation starts. Map and reduce operations are typically performed by the same physical processor. Number of map tasks and reduce tasks are configurable. Operations are provisioned near the data. Commodity hardware and storage. Runtime takes care of splitting and moving data for operations. Special distributed file system. Example: Hadoop Distributed File System and Hadoop Runtime. Hadoop is a software platform that lets one easily write and run applications that process vast amounts of data. The main features which makes Hadoop especially useful are Scalable, Economical, Efficient, Reliable.Facebook uses Hadoop to analyze user behavior and the effectiveness of ads on the site. The tech team at The New York Times rented computing power on Amazons cloud and used Hadoop to convert 11 million archived articles

5.2   Case Study

Healthcare Applications[12]: Healthcare scientific applications, such as body area network, require of deploying hundreds of interconnected sensors to monitor the health status of a host. One of the biggest challenges is the streaming data collected by all those sensors, which needs to be processed in real time. Follow up data analysis would normally involve moving the collected big data to a cloud data center for status reporting and record tracking purpose. Therefore, an efficient cloud platform with very elastic scaling capacity is needed to support such kind of real time streaming data applications.

Healthcare science has been consistently pushed forward by the advent of big data technology. Healthcare scientific applications usually involve streaming in-

put data generated by a large number of distributed sensors. Such data are
further sent to the state of art big data frameworks and platforms to process.
For example, the Body Area Network that is widely recognized as a medium to
access, monitor, and evaluate the real-time health status of a person, has long
been notorious for its computing intensiveness to process Gigabytes of data in
real time. Such data are collected from well configured sensors to sample the
real time signals of body temperature, blood pressure, respiratory and heart rate,
chest sound, and cardiovascular status, to name a few among others.

To process stream big-data in real time, traditional parallelized processing
frameworks, such as Hadoop MapReduce, Pregel, and Graphlab, are structurally
constrained and functionally limited. The major difficulty lies in their designs
are primarily contrived to access and process the static input data. No built
in iterative module can be used when the input data arrives in a stream flow.
Moreover, the existing frameworks are unable to handle the scenarios when the
streaming input datasets are from various sources and have different arrival rates.
Healthcare scientific applications vary the data acquisition frequency when the
behavior of the person changes. For example, the data collected when a person
is sleeping can be far less than the data collected when the person is running or
swimming.

5.3   MapReduce Model and Notations:

In this section,formulation of the real time tasks scheduling problem is presented, for analyse the scheduling performance in a theoretical way. A model is
created as (T,P,A) to describe real time task scheduling on a MapReduce method,
where T is the set of real time tasks, P the MapReduce method with processors
set, and A the scheduling algorithm.[10]

The task set is represented as T=$\{t_1, t_2, t_3, ..., t_n\}$, where n is number of tasks
running on MapReduce model. In real time systems this task set T represented
as(a_i, e_i, p_i), where a_i is the first release of task t_i, e_i is the worst case execution
time of t_i, p_i is the time period of task t_i, it is known that $e_i < p_i$.[10]

Now task representation in Real time MapReduce task, As a parallel programming model, MapReduce can automatically process massive data sets in a distributed fashion by breaking the processing into many small computations using two operators, 1. the map operation transforms the input into an intermediate representation, 2. the reduce operation combines the intermediate representation into the final output. A typical MapReduce model is shown in Fig5.1.[10]

A task t_i is divided into x modules, that x modules are given to x maps, on that x map y reduce operations are performed, the result of reduce operation is store in z output parts. Now take M_i as time taken to complete x map operations, R_i as time taken to complete y reduce operations. Now Real time MapReduce task represented as (a_i, M_i, R_i, p_i)[10]

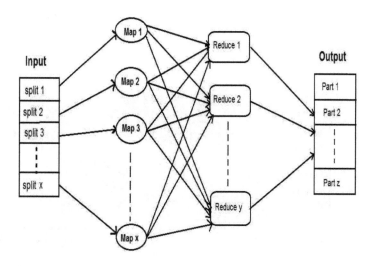

Figure 5.1: MapReduce programming models

In MapReduce method,The MapReduce-based cloud is a set of machines, P, running the MapReduce programming model, and thus, it is collectively referred to as a MapReduce cluster with a certain computing capability. The MapReduce programming model has several implementations, among which the open

57

source Hadoop is the most popular both in industry and academic institutions. The scheduling algorithm A is actually a set of rules for mapping a task from $T=\{t_1, t_2, t_3, ..., t_n\}$ onto the exclusive MapReduce cluster P.

5.4   MapReduce Word counting Example explanation

Consider the problem of counting the number of occurrences of each word in a large collection of documents. The steps for Mapreduce work as follow

Step 1: Divide collection of document among the class(splits)

Step 2: Class object gives count of individual word in document, repeat for all class objects in document.

Step 3: sum up the count from all object to give final output of document.

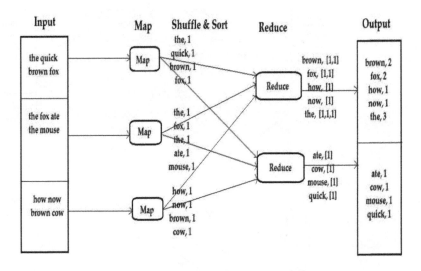

Figure 5.2: Word Count Execution Steps

Take a document having three statements as 1. the quick brown fox. 2. the fox ate the mouse. 3. how now brown cow. Now apply the Word count MapReduce on this document, the steps are shown in Fig.5.2.

Explanation: In First step document is dive into three class(statements). In second step map the statement as word and count value(as 1). In third step reduce of map words is done by counting words, in reduce step the words are divided into two set as {brown, fox, how, now, the} and {ate, cow, mouse, quick}. In final step output is presented as word and count.

5.5   Conclusion

This chapter having introduction of MapReduce, Healthcare Applications as case study, Mapreduce model and notations used and finally simple example of word count application using MapReduce method.

CHAPTER **6**

Thesis Conclusion

In thesis conclusion i discourse about my thesis contents as, A brief introduction of Real Time Systems, real time task scheduling and cloud computing,than case study, than related work, motivation and problem statement are presented in Chapter 1.

In chapter 2, we discussed real time system model, workload model ,Scheduling model, scheduling steps and other issues related to the real time task scheduling, and also discussed about performance parameters in scheduling of real time tasks.

In chapter 3 we have seen that Aperiodic tasks are scheduling by four scheduling algorithms BEDF, FFE, BFE and WFE. By simulation results it is shown that the three proposed algorithms always behaves better than that of Basic EDF in different performance parameter consideration.

In chapter 4 we have seen that Periodic tasks are scheduling by four scheduling algorithms BEDF, FFE, BFE and WFE. By simulation results it is shown that the three proposed algorithms always behaves better than that of Basic EDF in different performance parameter consideration.

In chapter 5 having introduction of MapReduce, Healthcare Applications as case study, Mapreduce model and notations used and finally simple example of word count application using MapReduce method.

CHAPTER 7

Future Work

In thesis the scheduling of Aperiodic tasks, Periodic tasks are done. In future work scheduling of Sporadic task will be done. Sporadic task is Real time task which is activated irregularly with some known bounded rate. The bounded rate is characterized by a minimum inter arrival period, that is, a minimum interval of time between two successive activations. The sporadic task is represented by a tuple (e_i, q_i, d_i) where e_i the worst case execution time, q_i denotes the minimum separation between two consecutive instances of t_i, d_i is the relative deadline.

In chapter 5 the brief description of the real time task scheduling and MapReduce is presented. In future work more discussion about the MapReduce and try to apply a new approach on reduce step, such that new approach will work better.

Bibliography

[1] EKELIN, C., "Clairvoyant non-preemptive edf scheduling," in *Real-Time Systems, 2006. 18th Euromicro Conference on*, pp. 7–pp, IEEE, 2006.

[2] HARITSA, J. R., LIVNY, M., and CAREY, M. J., "Earliest deadline scheduling for real-time database systems," in *Real-Time Systems Symposium, 1991. Proceedings., Twelfth*, pp. 232–242, IEEE, 1991.

[3] LI, H., *Scheduling mixed-criticality real-time systems*. PhD thesis, University of North Carolina at Chapel Hill, 2013.

[4] LIU, S., QUAN, G., and REN, S., "On-line scheduling of real-time services for cloud computing," in *Services (SERVICES-1), 2010 6th World Congress on*, pp. 459–464, IEEE, 2010.

[5] OH, S.-H. and YANG, S.-M., "A modified least-laxity-first scheduling algorithm for real-time tasks," in *Real-Time Computing Systems and Applications, 1998. Proceedings. Fifth International Conference on*, pp. 31–36, IEEE, 1998.

[6] SAHOO, B. and EKKA, A. A., "Backward fault recovery in real time distributed system of periodic task with timing and precedence constrain," *Proceedings of the International Conference on Emerging Trends in High Performance Architecture, Algorithms and Computing, July*, pp. 11–13, 2007.

[7] SANTHOSH, R. and RAVICHANDRAN, T., "Pre-emptive scheduling of online real time services with task migration for cloud computing," in *Pattern Recognition, Informatics and Mobile Engineering (PRIME), 2013 International Conference on*, pp. 271–276, IEEE, 2013.

[8] SHARMA, R. and OTHERS, "Task migration with edf-rm scheduling algorithms in distributed system," in *Advances in Computing and Communications (ICACC), 2012 International Conference on*, pp. 182–185, IEEE, 2012.

[9] SHIN, K. G. and RAMANATHAN, P., "Real-time computing: A new discipline of computer science and engineering," *Proceedings of the IEEE*, vol. 82, no. 1, pp. 6–24, 1994.

[10] TENG, F., MAGOULÈS, F., YU, L., and LI, T., "A novel real-time scheduling algorithm and performance analysis of a mapreduce-based cloud," *The Journal of Supercomputing*, vol. 69, no. 2, pp. 739–765, 2014.

[11] YANG, L., ZHU, X., CHEN, H., WANG, J., YIN, S., and LIU, X., "Real-time tasks oriented energy-aware scheduling in virtualized clouds," 2014.

[12] ZHANG, F., CAO, J., KHAN, S. U., LI, K., and HWANG, K., "A task-level adaptive mapreduce framework for real-time streaming data in healthcare applications," *Future Generation Computer Systems*, vol. 43, pp. 149–160, 2015.